Grassroot Institute of Hawaii
Policy Brief, December 2023

How to facilitate more homebuilding in Hawaii

Changes to Hawaii's zoning codes are essential and can be effected at no cost to Hawaii taxpayers

By Jonathan Helton

Letter from the President

Keiʻi Akina, Ph.D.
President and CEO
Grassroot Institute of Hawaii

Dear Reader,

Believe it or not, it is possible for Hawaii's state and county officials to start solving our housing crisis without spending a penny on taxpayer-funded projects.

Too often, lawmakers focus on big, sweeping solutions – such as government-funded housing projects. But what we really need to do is reconsider the many smaller policies that have compounded to cause Hawaii's housing crisis in the first place.

By now, it is common knowledge that Hawaii has the most homebuilding-related regulations in the nation. In this report, we explore how removing or reforming some of those could yield big results.

Our recommendations include allowing more multifamily homes; reducing lot-sizes, setback requirements and floor area ratios; expanding mixed-use zoning; implementing "by right" approvals; reducing or abolishing parking minimums; allowing more accessory dwelling units; and repurposing commercial buildings for residential use.

The key is to remove unnecessary roadblocks that stand in the way of a vibrant and healthy housing market, however small they might seem.

And adopting such changes has been proven around the world to facilitate the creation of more housing – at a lower cost for homebuyers and at no cost to taxpayers. That's what I would call a win-win.

When it comes to housing, the best way to serve the people of Hawaii is to make it easier to build homes.

E hana kākou (Let's work together),

Keli'i Akina, Ph.D.

GRASSROOT
INSTITUTE OF HAWAII

Prepared by Grassroot Institute of Hawaii. ISBN: 9798870510644.

Grassroot Institute of Hawaii
1050 Bishop St. #508
Honolulu, Hawaii 96813
808-864-1776
info@grassrootinstitute.org

Jonathan Helton is a policy researcher at the Grassroot Institute of Hawaii.

Photos by Charley Myers
Layout and design by klworks.net

Table of Contents

Executive summary

This report highlights ways that state and county policymakers could easily and inexpensively boost the supply of housing in Hawaii's urban areas, primarily by streamlining homebuilding regulations.

Proposed measures include "upzoning" lands in the state's urban land-use districts to allow multiunit housing and smaller lot construction, promoting adaptive reuse, legalizing mixed-use structures, adopting by-right approvals, repealing parking minimums, encouraging accessory dwelling units and authorizing self-certification for building permits.

Introduction

Hawaii's housing crisis is acute — so much so that in July 2023, the state's governor declared it an emergency and suspended dozens of laws with the intent of making it easier to build homes.

Gov. Josh Green has since reinstated some of the key laws that make homebuilding in Hawaii so time-consuming, costly and difficult. But the point was still made that legislative action is required if Hawaii is to produce enough homes to meet demand.

According to the state Department of Business, Economic Development and Tourism, Hawaii needs about 3,600 new housing units a year to keep up with statewide housing demand through 2030.[1]

Unfortunately, not everyone agrees about how to achieve that goal — as shown by how little progress state and county lawmakers have made through the years in facilitating more housing supply.

If anything, both state and county lawmakers have tended to exacerbate the housing crisis with more layers of regulations, fees and taxes. That's one reason Gov. Green went ahead with his unilateral decree to sweep away red tape.

In fact, most of the laws he initially suspended provided a good blueprint for what state legislators could enact into law permanently. And, since state emergency orders do eventually expire, the housing crisis will continue if state and county policymakers do not act quickly.

In an effort to accelerate state and county legislative action, this report focuses on regulatory reforms that could increase housing supply and affordability in areas of Hawaii that have already been designated as urban by the state Land Use Commission.

Indeed, most housing in Hawaii is on urban lands, but not all urban lands are zoned by the counties for housing. This report outlines how the state and counties could easily expand homebuilding on urban lands — at virtually no expense to taxpayers.

If anything, both state and county lawmakers have tended to exacerbate the housing crisis with more layers of regulations, fees and taxes.

Reforms that would encourage more homebuilding

Many Hawaii residents want to "Keep the country country," but that is less likely to happen if policymakers continue to prohibit or discourage homebuilding in Hawaii's existing urban cores – namely Honolulu, Kailua, Kaneohe, Aiea and Kapolei on Oahu; Kahului and Kihei on Maui; Lihue on Kauai; and Kona and Hilo on Hawaii Island.

To encourage homebuilding in Hawaii's urban cores, policymakers need to pass laws that allow:

- Upzoning, which typically involves smaller lot construction, reduced setbacks, increased floor area ratios and lot-splitting.

- "Adaptive reuse" of existing office, retail or commercial buildings.

- Fewer mandated parking spaces.

- More accessory dwelling units.

- Mixed-use zoning.

- By-right approvals.

- Greater use of self-certification in permitting.

These actions might not have an immediate affect on Hawaii's housing prices, but they would expand the housing stock available to families and individuals, which could help stabilize or even possibly lower home prices in the long term.[2]

Upzoning

Upzoning refers to allowing denser forms of housing, such as duplexes and triplexes, to be built on parcels that were previously zoned for less-dense housing, such as single-family homes.

The purpose of upzoning is to increase the number of housing units on land that is already zoned for urban use, including residential.

Table 1: Percent of lands in each Land Use Commission district, by island, 2023[3]				
	Urban	**Conservation**	**Agricultural**	**Rural**
Total	4.88	48.00	46.86	0.27
Hawaii	2.10	50.69	47.16	0.05
Kauai	4.19	56.17	39.29	0.35
Lanai	3.76	42.21	51.37	2.66
Maui	5.16	41.83	52.11	0.90
Molokai	1.53	30.02	67.33	1.13
Oahu	26.34	40.60	33.07	0.00

If Hawaii's counties upzoned single-family parcels throughout their urban cores, the resulting increase in housing supply would likely cause home prices to fall or stabilize.

The city of Auckland in New Zealand has seen positive results from implementing this policy. In 2016, the city upzoned three-quarters of its residential land as a part of its Auckland Unitary Plan.[4] The plan ended single-family-only zones and allowed more multifamily housing. A spate of studies analyzing this change has found that it increased housing supply and lowered housing prices.[5]

In the U.S., cities such as Minneapolis and Portland have likewise taken steps to allow denser housing.[6] An Urban Institute study of housing in the U.S. found that "reforms that loosen restrictions are associated with a statistically significant 0.8% increase in housing supply within three to nine years of reform passage."

Hawaii housing prices might not respond in exactly the same way as anywhere else due to a number of factors, but policymakers could at least expect upzoning to increase housing supply and affect housing prices in a positive manner.

Allow smaller lots

Each county has minimum lot size requirements that vary slightly depending on the zoning of the parcels. Table 2 displays the typical lot minimums for a variety of housing types.

Table 2: Typical minimum lot sizes in Hawaii, in square feet, 2023[7]			
County	Detached single-family	Duplex	Apartment and multifamily
Hawaii	7,500	7,500	7,500
Honolulu	3,500	3,500	7,500
Maui	6,000	7,500	10,000
Kauai	6,000	10,000	10,000

The main point of minimum lot sizes — along with setbacks and floor area ratios — is to ensure that each house has a yard of a certain size. However, since land values in Hawaii are so high, mandating that a certain amount of land around each house be devoted to yard space guarantees higher housing prices.[8]

Minimum lot sizes also encourage developers to build larger houses instead of smaller starter homes that could be affordable to more people.[9]

Faced with having to provide a certain amount of land for each home, it makes logical sense that many homebuilders would build the largest houses allowable to maximize their profitability. If smaller lots were allowed, thus reducing project costs, homebuilders would find it financially feasible to build smaller, less expensive homes.

If smaller lots were allowed, thus reducing project costs, homebuilders would find it financially feasible to build smaller, less expensive homes.

The positive effect of this reform has played out in Houston, where in 1998 the city lowered its minimum lot sizes for the city core from 5,000 square feet to 1,400 square feet, then in 2013 lowered lot sizes for non-core areas. Research has found that these changes increased construction and decreased the average size of homes in Houston, benefitting lower- and middle-income earners the most.[10]

Reduce setbacks

Zoning setbacks mandate how far back a dwelling can be built from the front, side and sometimes back of the lot. Large setbacks establish a greater distance between the dwelling and the lot line, which can make for a nice yard but serve to limit the amount and size of dwelling units on the property.[11] Smaller setback requirements, on the other hand, can provide more room for actual living areas.

Table 3: Typical setbacks for a detached single family dwelling, in square feet, 2023[12]

County	Front	Side	Rear	Width
Hawaii	15	8	15	60
Honolulu	10	5	5	50
Maui	15	6	6	60
Kauai	10	5	5	60

Increase floor area ratios

Floor area ratios, which refer to the size of a building in relation to the parcel of land on which it sits, can also have a tremendous impact on what kind of structures can be built. For example, a FAR of 1.0 allows a single-story dwelling to take up the entire lot, while a FAR of 0.5 allows it to take up half of the lot.[13] In Honolulu's residential zones, the FAR cannot exceed 0.7.[14]

Allow lot-splitting

Lot-splitting, also called subdividing, is the process of dividing a parcel into two or more lots. Allowing Hawaii homeowners to divide their parcels into two or more lots without too much expense or regulatory hassle would boost the state's housing stock while providing original homeowners with a new avenue to build their wealth.

California's SB9 could serve as a model for lot-splitting and other zoning reform in Hawaii, although it is not perfect.[15] The 2021 state law mandates that most areas zoned for single-homes are eligible for lot-splitting. Landowners can legally divide their lots in two, provided that the newly created lots meet minimum size standards. The law also prohibits local governments from using zoning rules such as setbacks to make it impossible for landowners to split their lot.

Daniel Herriges, editor-in-chief of the city reform advocacy group Strong Towns based in Minnesota, wrote that lot-splitting "amounts to a hack on our existing financing and building culture and institutions."[16]

Furthermore, the Seattle-based Sightline Institute explained that, "On many sites, lot splits can help solve one of the biggest problems with small-scale infill: how to get a construction loan."

Sightline said many banks and credit unions "struggle to figure out how to value a lot with an extra rental on site, and therefore can't always offer good loan terms to people looking to build a backyard cottage or remodel into a duplex. But every lender knows exactly how to value a little lot with a new house on it."[17]

Creating homes through lot-splitting could give existing Hawaii homeowners the money they need to put their children through college, or dissuade them from moving to the mainland.

California's law has not resulted in much land-splitting to date, but researchers at the University of California at Berkeley attribute that to a combination of local government resistance to SB9 initiatives and state-level incentives for accessory dwelling unit construction.

The researchers recommended revisiting the owner-occupancy standards for lot-splitting, creating clear guidelines for lot splitting and other SB9 projects, and reforming state construction-defect liability laws.[18]

Hawaii lawmakers should learn from SB9's reforms and build on it to create a successful lot-splitting law that encourages vibrant neighborhoods.

Adaptive reuse

Adaptive reuse, or AR, refers to the conversion of existing buildings from one primary use to another.

Around the world, cities are grappling with higher-than-normal commercial vacancy rates in their downtown office buildings, which has led them to question whether converting office spaces to apartments could help increase their supply of housing.[19]

According to Colliers, a Toronto-based commercial real estate services company, this trend includes Honolulu.[20]

Already, Oahu developers have converted or are in the process of converting old office, hotel and commercial buildings to create residential housing units and new commercial spaces.

The Hocking Hale in Chinatown, at the corner of North King Street and Nuuanu Avenue, is just one example.[21] According to the Honolulu Star-Advertiser in July 2021, a development firm led in part by state Rep. Mark Hashem planned to spend $27 million converting the three-story building into 40 apartments.[22]

In addition, Christine Camp's Avalon Group is working to retrofit the Davies Pacific Center to contain mostly condos,[23] and other homebuilders are eyeing additional downtown buildings for conversion.[24]

Adaptive reuse benefits

Reusing existing buildings for new purposes is an attractive proposition for many reasons. First, there can be environmental benefits.

According to the Central City Association of Los Angeles, adaptive reuse projects "are generally more sustainable than new construction because they typically require fewer construction materials and inputs that are associated with higher carbon emissions, like the making and transporting of concrete and steel or the removal of demolition debris."[25]

According to CCALA, it can take between 50 and 80 years for a new energy-efficient building to recover the energy lost from all the building materials destroyed when demolishing an existing structure.[26]

Adaptive reuse also can help preserve cultural and historical structures. The conversion of the Queen Emma Building in Honolulu is a good example.

In some cases, adaptive reuse can simply be less expensive than tearing down an old building and putting up a new one.

Constructed in 1964, the 12-story building was originally used for office space. But after it sat vacant for some time, a group of designers and developers decided to convert it to a residential building. Work on the project began in 2018 and finished in 2020.[27]

"Buildings we have seen all our lives can provide affordable housing while retaining the character of our neighborhoods," housing advocate Renee Ing wrote in Honolulu Civil Beat in December 2022.[28]

In some cases, adaptive reuse can simply be less expensive than tearing down an old building and putting up a new one.

A study by researchers from the RAND Corp. found that construction costs for adaptive reuse projects in Los Angeles were as much as 48% lower than new construction. Total development costs, which included financing, engineering costs and architectural services, were 27% less for AR projects. The authors did express that these estimates were just

that — estimates — and that "caution in interpreting this evidence is warranted."[29]

On the mainland, Los Angeles stands out as a city with a successful AR policy. The city's AR ordinance has been credited with adding 12,000 units to its downtown area since it was adopted in 1999.[30]

Changes that would facilitate adaptive reuse

In a 2021 white paper, the Central City Association of Los Angeles said LA's adaptive-reuse ordinance succeeded because the city:

- Allowed buildings to change uses from commercial to residential "by right" — that is, automatically – without going before a council or commission where the project could be voted up or down.

- Exempted AR projects from California Environmental Quality Act review.

- Relaxed parking and loading-space mandates.

- Allowed one-story rooftop additions automatically.

- Added a new building code section to specify requirements for AR projects.[31]

These policy changes enabled builders to bypass regulations that would have held up their efforts to create new housing or otherwise find new uses for existing buildings.

According to the aforementioned RAND study: "These changes provided a significant and successful incentive to redevelop many buildings in [downtown LA] over several years after the policy was passed."[32]

Additionally, urban planners William Riggs and Forrest Chamberlain wrote in the journal Sustainable Cities and Society in 2018 that LA's ordinance "appears to have accelerated downtown development activity, reversing development trends and potentially providing an additional tool for developers during economic lulls."[33]

Adaptive reuse limitations

Of course, not all buildings are suitable for adaptive reuse. Reasons include a building's age, architectural layout and whether it has any structural flaws that need repair.

Researchers from the Terner Center for Housing Innovation in Berkley, California, noted in 2021 that buildings especially conducive to AR are ones with "specific architectural characteristics such as shallow floor plates, generous exterior exposure or unique building features."[34]

If Hawaii's counties were to adopt AR ordinances modeled after LA's policy, it would by no means fix Hawaii's housing crisis. But an "all of the above" approach to housing construction that streamlines homebuilding regulations in urban areas likely would encourage AR projects wherever possible.

Parking reform

Parking mandates generally specify that each home, commercial establishment or civic building must have a minimum number of parking spaces.

The number is usually determined by either a set amount or as a function of the square footage of the buildings.

Table 4: Hawaii parking stall minimums for select unit types, by county, 2023[35]			
County	2,000 sqft single-family home	2,000 sqft duplex	1,000 sqft apartment unit
Hawaii	2	2	1.25
Honolulu	2	2	1
Maui	2	2	2
Kauai	2	2	2

The impact of parking minimums

The biggest issue with parking mandates is the opportunity costs they impose on homebuilders. Land in urban areas is often highly valuable, since it can be used to construct housing or business space in close proximity to other amenities.

In downtown Honolulu, property values hover near $20 million an acre.[36] By forcing land to be used for parking instead of housing or other uses, cities hamstring business opportunities, reduce economic activity and drive up housing costs.

In 2020, the Ulupono Initiative estimated that building a parking garage in downtown Honolulu could cost as much as $57,000 per parking space, while constructing a single parking space for a residential unit could cost $22,500.[37]

Builders on neighbor islands can expect similar costs because lower land values are offset by more expensive materials.

High construction costs for parking can add between $5,000 and $77,000 to the price of each housing unit, depending on the land costs and carrying costs for the development, which are likely to be higher in urban core areas.[38]

Parking mandates also take up space that could go toward building more housing, which illustrates the trade-offs involved in requiring certain amounts of parking.

To put these costs into perspective, consider that the average parking stall of 320 square feet is just slightly smaller than a small studio unit.[39] For every parking stall built, then, there is one less housing unit.

Finally, parking minimums drain city coffers of tax revenue. Land used for parking could be used for homes or businesses – a much more valuable use in terms of property taxes.[40]

Parking reform gaining momentum

Partially in response to the Ulupono study, Honolulu officials abolished or lowered several of the city's parking mandates in 2020. These reductions applied mainly to areas that were in the so-called primary

urban center and near bus stops or rail stations.[41]

Parking reform is also gaining momentum on the mainland with many cities scrapping parking requirements completely, and many others decreasing them for certain areas.[42]

Hawaii's county governments should follow suit and abolish all of their parking requirements. If county officials determine this is not politically feasible, they could at least reduce parking requirements or abolish them for certain urban core areas as Honolulu has done.

'Where will I park?'

The common objection to parking reform is, "Where will I park?"

One answer is that individuals who want to have places to park their vehicles could buy or rent housing that has parking. If demand for parking spaces exists, homebuilders would no doubt strive to meet it – albeit at a higher cost, which those who want parking should be willing to pay.

Similarly, those who do not want parking – or who want fewer spaces than are currently required – would

No minimum parking requirement (Requirement in the Primary Urban Center, Kapolei, and Ewa)

January 2020
Map is subject to change.

have the option to avoid the higher costs that parking minimums entail.

Of course, some people who need access to a car might not be able to afford an apartment with ample parking. But, in a sense, that is a reflection on the shortage of housing in urban areas. As writer Daniel Herriges of Strong Towns wrote in August 2023:

"The fact that people who really, really need a reliable parking spot – something that is genuinely true of a subset of low-income people – feel forced to take an apartment in a building without any parking is a consequence of both the overall housing shortage and the way we have restricted new building to a monoculture."[43]

Ultimately, though, the point is to offer more affordable housing options for residents who don't have a need for parking spaces. And studies do indicate that residents who live in areas with fewer parking spaces often own fewer cars and drive less.[44]

As a result, people who live in neighborhoods could choose to carpool to work, take the bus or rail, catch a ride with companies such as Uber or Lyft, rent a car as needed or even contract with others to share a parking space.

Furthermore, parking reform ideally would be paired with mixed-use zoning reform to allow neighborhood businesses to pop up, which could turn a short drive to the coffee shop or grocery store into a walk.

Indeed, many of Hawaii's older neighborhoods – such as Kaimuki, Haleiwa, Lihue, Hilo and Hana – were built before parking minimums. Today, these neighborhoods draw tourists and locals alike for their community, walkability and mom and pop businesses. Changing parking minimums and other zoning requirements could allow for the creation of a 21st century version of these traditional, tight-knit neighborhoods.

The reality is that people can solve all sorts of problems when governments simply get out of the way. In Hawaii's case, that means removing land-use and zoning laws that hinder housing growth and urban evolution.

Accessory dwelling units

The Maui County zoning code defines an accessory dwelling unit as "an attached or detached dwelling unit which is incidental or subordinate to the main or principal dwelling on a lot."[45] Also called supplemental dwelling units or "ohana units,"[46] ADUs are partly intended to provide housing for elderly family members.

In 2014, the Hawaii Appleseed Center for Law and Economic Justice advocated greater use of ADUs, stating: "Our population is also rapidly aging, while young people are often hard-pressed to afford the high cost of living in Hawaii."[47]

Accessory dwellings have been legal at the state level since 1981. In 1989, however, the state passed that authority to the counties after some community members complained about the size of ADUs.[48]

In 1993, Honolulu banned ADUs from being used as long-term rentals,[49] which contributed to a decline in people building them.[50]

In 1994, Hawaii County imposed stringent minimum lot size, height and permit application rules that helped freeze ADU construction.[52] Before that, however, ADUs had proved popular on the island, with production peaking at 581 units in 1991.[53]

In 2015, the Honolulu City Council and then-Mayor Kirk Caldwell enacted Bill 20, which lifted the city's ban on rental ADUs.[54]

As Figure 1 shows, legalization resulted in a significant increase in the number of ADU permits issued by the Honolulu Department of Planning and Permitting.

Outside of Hawaii, these little dwellings have produced big results in places that have legalized and encouraged their construction.

Evidence from Seattle, Portland and Vancouver, Canada, suggests that ADUs are often rented to tenants at below-median rents, making them a form of affordable housing.[55] These below-average rents might benefit primarily friends and family of the owners of the primary dwellings, but ADUs nonetheless boost the overall housing stock.[56]

Figure 1: Time series of Honolulu ADU permits[51]

ADU rentals allowed

To promote ADUs, Hawaii's counties could:

- Remove any language from their statues that require landowners to live in either the main dwellings or the ADUs. Whatever the reason might have been for adopting this language, the practical effect has been to constrain the rental market.

Yale University law professor Anika Singh Lemar asserted in a 2022 report that "owner-occupancy requirements are back-door attempts to block renters"[57] because properties with an ADU can only give rise to one rental unit instead of two, and properties with rental homes cannot add an ADU.

As Lemar wrote in that report:

"These owner-occupancy rules have several negative effects on equity, efforts to build multi-family housing, and the overall housing supply. Because renters typically have lower incomes than homeowners and are racially more diverse, owner-occupancy requirements affect the economic and demographic makeup of neighborhoods. Owner-occupancy requirements also prevent property owners from developing repeat expertise in acquiring and renovating existing housing stock to add ADUs; as a result, lenders are less likely to finance ADUs."

ADUs might not be right for everyone, but they are easier to build and less expensive than a brand new, full-size single-family home or duplex.

- Allow existing, unpermitted accessory structures to be permitted as ADUs. Doing this would give a legal reprieve to homeowners who built structures years ago without building permits. These unpermitted structures pose a problem for property assessments and sales to new buyers, so grandfathering in these existing structures could also benefit the public at large by boosting the housing stock.

- Adjust parking minimums, minimum lot size and setback requirements to accommodate the addition of more ADUs.

Table 5: Hawaii minimum lot sizes for ADUs by county	
County	Minimum
Hawaii	10,000 sqft
Honolulu	3,500 sqft
Maui	6,000 sqft
Kauai	6,000 sqft

- Publish pre-approved ADU plans to make it easier for county permitting departments to review and approve ADU permit applications. Numerous cities in California now offer such plans.[58]

- Waive city fees or provide other financial incentives. In 2016, Honolulu waived building permit, sewer and other fees up to $10,000 and offered a fee rebate to homeowners who had already built an ADU after the 2015 legalization. The purpose of the ordinance was to avoid the charges that made building an ADU cost prohibitive for many.[59]

Kauai also waives building permit fees, sewer connection charges and a host of other fees for people who agree to rent their "additional rental units" at an affordable rate for five years.[60] Kauai's additional rental units are similar to ADUs, which are also legal in the county. The major difference between the two is that additional rental units must be rented or occupied for a certain number of months per year.[61]

Likewise, Maui enacted an "Ohana assistance program" earlier this year. The program offers homeowners up to county-funded grants to construct ADUs on their properties, with the condition that they be used as long-term rentals.[62]

ADUs might not be right for everyone, but they are easier to build and less expensive than a brand new, full-size single-family home or duplex, and are a convenient way to house older or younger family members and build intergenerational wealth for the primary homeowners.

Mixed-use zoning

Mixed-use zoning allows both residential and commercial uses in the same building and on the same block.

Mixed-use buildings were common in all pre-automobile cities. It was normal for watchmakers, bakers, lawyers and all sorts of other business people to live in the same buildings in which they worked. Their stores or offices were usually on the bottom floors, and their living quarters were typically on the floor or floors above or in an apartment in back.[63]

With the advent of automobiles, people no longer had to live in close proximity to where they worked, and many moved to newly developed suburbs surrounding the cities. This was later dubbed "urban sprawl."

In recent years, there has been a push against urban sprawl in favor of housing built closer to businesses and transit. The benefits of this traditional development style could be far-reaching.

First, if neighborhoods were more walkable, fewer people would use their cars,[64] which would mean less traffic, less air pollution and less wear and tear on city streets. Also, residents who give up on driving likely would save money on gas, repairs, insurance and other car-related expenses.

For example, the cost of owning a vehicle in Hawaii is roughly $8,100 a year, according to a 2021 study commissioned by the Ulupono Initiative.[65] Meanwhile, annual bus passes cost far less – $880 in Honolulu,[66] $540 on Maui,[67] $550 on Kauai[68] and free on Hawaii Island.[69]

If neighborhoods were more walkable, fewer people would use their cars, which would mean less traffic, less air pollution and less wear and tear on city streets.

Second, studies show that walkable neighborhoods also yield positive health outcomes. People lose weight, cardiovascular disease declines, and people report being happier.[70]

Policies that could help Hawaii's counties revert to the more traditional mixed-use development model include:

- Legalizing grocery stores, barber shops, daycares, doctor offices and similar small retail uses in existing residential zones, with appropriate safeguards in place for nuisances such as noise.

- Relaxing restrictions on home-based businesses. This could include allowing reasonably sized signage and allowing a small number of staff who do not live at the home. Counties could also remove language that limits the number of customers who can visit a home-based business on a given day, as well as unclear language concerning the effect of the business on the "character" of the dwelling.[71]

- Allowing residential uses in all existing business-related zones. Such residential uses should not be limited to either the ground floor or floors above the ground floor; all floors should be available for use as dwelling units. This would promote walkability in existing commercial areas.

By-right approvals

Much of this report has focused on what policymakers should allow to be built, but there is also the question of how building plans that meet all existing codes should be approved. One of the most important reforms the state Legislature or Hawaii's counties could adopt is what's known as ministerial or by-right zoning.

These terms refer to projects that can proceed automatically without discretionary approval from a neighborhood board, planning department, planning commission or county council.

Researchers with the Economic Research Organization at the University of Hawai'i have pointed out that by-right approvals give homebuilders greater certainty that their projects can proceed, and often quicken the homebuilding process.[72]

Honolulu's duplex law is a good example of by-right zoning. The county's zoning code allows duplexes to be built wherever single-family homes are legal.[73] Homeowners wanting to convert their single-family homes into duplexes do not need permit approval from the Honolulu Department of Planning and Permitting.[74]

Minimizing the number of discretionary approvals and maximizing the number of automatically approved uses would speed up homebuilding and foster entrepreneurship.

Maui's duplex law, on the other hand, requires someone looking to construct a duplex in a residential zone to receive a special-use permit, which requires an application and a discretionary review by the county planning commission.[75]

Despite this drawback, Maui's law is an improvement over what had been the case. Prior to March 2023, duplexes were not allowed in residential districts at all, or at least not without going through a significantly longer approval process.[76]

By-right zoning should not be limited to duplexes. It should extend to other types of dwellings, lot-splitting, home-based businesses and adaptive reuse. Minimizing the number of discretionary approvals and maximizing the number of automatically approved uses would speed up homebuilding and foster entrepreneurship.

Self-certification in permitting

Hawaii's approval and permitting delays are among the worst in the country, according to the Economic Research Organization at the University of Hawai'i.[77] Time is money in homebuilding, as in most business situations, so delays add to the cost of housing.

A 2011 study by economist Paul Emrath for the National Association of Homebuilders discovered that delays, including those caused by waiting for a building permit, increase the sales price of new homes by 1.7% on average.[78]

One way to speed up the permitting process would be to allow what is called self-certification – a process by which architects, engineers and other professionals are allowed to self-approve building permits for certain projects.

These professionals become liable for certain aspects of the permit, but the benefit is that homeowners and small businesses do not have to wait months for a permit to complete basic repairs.

In Honolulu, a self-certification program was debated and eventually adopted in late 2023. While vetting the bill, some people expressed concern that self-certification could lead to illegal or hazardous buildings being constructed.[79] However, cities across the country – such as North Las Vegas, Chicago, Phoenix and New York City – have been using self-certification with great success.[80]

Hawaii's approval and permitting delays are among the worst in the country.

For self-certification to work properly and safely in Hawaii, policymakers could limit it to only certain types of building permits. Complex projects, such as new high-rises, could still be subject to some degree of county review. The installation of a new deck, however, should be within the realm of self-certification.

Honolulu's self-certification program, for example, applies only to Department of Hawaiian Home Lands projects, commercial tenant improvements and affordable rental projects.[81]

Hawaii counties could also conduct random audits of self-certified plans. New York City has employed some degree of self-certification since 1975, with an expansion taking place in 1995.[82] The city does, however, audit building plans submitted by professional certifiers. According to the 2023 New York City Mayor's Management Report, city auditors randomly review roughly 20% of self-certified permits to deter cheating.[83]

Finally, there should be consequences for self-reviewers who vouch for illegal building plans. If their violations reach a certain threshold, their self-certification privileges should be revoked, as is done in the cities that already allow the practice.[84] In addition, violators should face some degree of liability if anyone is physically harmed by a flaw in the plans they approved.

All of these measures would help ensure that self-certification is used safely.

Furthermore, it is difficult to see how self-certification would result in more problems than the status quo, considering the county planning departments already sometimes approve or do not properly vet out-of-code home designs.[85]

Conclusion

The state's lawmakers will not be able to resolve Hawaii's housing crisis without removing or liberalizing existing policies that have long hindered homebuilding in the islands.

The reforms proposed in this report do not comprise an exhaustive list, but rather are only a sampling of land-use, zoning and permitting changes that could reduce the state's astronomical housing prices to help prospective Hawaii homeowners realize their goal of homeownership.

Ultimately, zoning reforms intended to increase housing supply should be applied in a comprehensive fashion. For example, it would be difficult to allow more duplexes without changing the minimum lot-size requirements, floor area ratios and setbacks.

These needed changes will not happen overnight. The policymaking process takes time, as does constructing physical housing units. That's why housing reform should be a priority. The sooner lawmakers act, the sooner housing in Hawaii can become more plentiful and less expensive.

Endnotes

1 "Hawaii Housing Demand: 2020-2030," Hawaii Department of Business, Economic Development and Tourism, Research and Economic Analysis Division, December 2019, p. 2.
2 Daniel Herriges, "What Would Mass Upzoning *Actually* Do to Property Values?" Strong Towns, Jan. 19, 2022; and Daniel Herriges, "Upzoning Might Not Lower Housing Costs. Do It Anyway." Strong Towns, April 26, 2023.
3 "Table 6.04 – Estimated Acreage of Land Use Districts, By Island: 2020 To 2022," 2022 State of Hawaii Data Book, accessed Nov. 8, 2023.
4 "What is the Auckland Unitary Plan?" Auckland Council, accessed April 25, 2023.
5 Ryan Greenaway-McGrevy, Gail Pacheco and Kade Sorensen, "The effect of upzoning on house prices and redevelopment premiums in Auckland, New Zealand," Urban Studies, 2021, pp. 960-961; and Ryan Greenaway-McGrevy, "Evaluating the Long-Run Effects of Zoning Reform on Urban Development," Economic Policy Centre, March 2023, p. 4.
6 Scott Beyer, "America's Upzoning Bills Are Already Creating More Housing," Independent Institute, Feb. 28, 2022.
7 Hawaii County Code, Section 25-5-7. Minimum yards, Section 25-5-24. Minimum building site area and Section 25-5-34, Minimum building site area, accessed Oct. 10, 2023; Revised Ordinances of Honolulu, § 21-3.70-1 Residential uses and development standards and § 21-3.90-1 Apartment mixed-use district uses and development standards, accessed Oct. 10, 2023; Maui Code of Ordinances, 19.08.040 – Area regulations, 19.10.050 – Development standards and 19.12.050 – Development standards, accessed Oct. 10, 2023; and Kauai County Code, Sec. 8-4.4 Development Standards for Residential Structures Which Involve the Subdivision of Land, accessed Oct. 10, 2023. Note that Kauai's minimum lot sizes as presented in this table apply to only structures built using subdivision of land. Kauai has separate standards for residences that are not built using subdivision, which are explained here: Kauai County Code, § 8-4.3 Development Standards for Residential Structures Not Involving the Subdivision of Land, accessed Oct. 24, 2023.
8 Nolan Gray, "Do Minimum Lot Size Rules Matter?" Strong Towns, June 20, 2019.
9 Jonathan Rothwell, "Land Use Politics, Housing Costs, and Segregation in California Cities," Terner Center for Housing Innovation, Sept. 5, 2019.
10 Salim Furth, "Resources for Reformers: Houston's minimum lot sizes," Market Urbanism, March 14, 2023.
11 Andrew Price, "The Problem with Setbacks," Strong Towns, Oct. 25, 2017.
12 Hawaii County Code, Section 25-5-7. Minimum yards, accessed Nov. 8, 2023; Revised Ordinances of Honolulu, § 21-3.70-1 Residential uses and development standards, accessed Nov. 8, 2023; Maui Code of Ordinances, 19.08.040 – Area regulations and 19.08.060 - Yards, accessed Nov. 8, 2023; and Kauai County Code, Sec. 8-4.4 Development Standards for Residential Structures Which Involve the Subdivision of Land, accessed Nov. 8, 2023. Note that Kauai's setbacks as presented in this table apply only to structures built using subdivision of land. Kauai has separate standards for residences that are not built using subdivision, which are explained here: Kauai County Code, § 8-4.3 Development Standards for Residential Structures Not Involving the Subdivision of Land, accessed Nov. 8, 2023.
13 Daniel Herriges, "What kind of city do we want to leave for our children?" Strong Towns, Sept. 23, 2020.
14 Revised Ordinances of Honolulu, § 21-3.70-1 Residential uses and development standards., accessed Oct. 26, 2023.
15 "Is SB 9 Working? Here's What Early Data Reveals," California YIMBY, Feb. 22, 2023.
16 Daniel Herriges, "The Secret Sauce (Maybe) of California's Zoning Reform," Strong Towns, Sept. 29, 2021.
17 Michael Andersen, "Five lessons from California's big zoning reform," Sightline Institute, Aug. 26, 2021.
18 David Garcia and Muhammad Alameldin, "California's HOME Act Turns One: Data and Insights from the First Year of Senate Bill 9," Terner Center for Housing Innovation at UC Berkeley, Jan. 18, 2023; and Muhammad Alameldin and David Garcia, "State Law, Local Interpretation: How Cities Are Implementing Senate Bill 9," Terner Center for Housing Innovation at UC Berkeley, June 8, 2022.
19 Janice Endresen, "Adaptive Reuse: Is Converting Empty Office Space to Housing Viable?" SC Johnson College of Business, Cornell University, July 6, 2023.
20 Mike Hamasu, "Office Market Takes A Step Backward," Colliers, April 30, 2023.
21 Alison Chiu, "Adaptive Reuse: New Life for Old Buildings," Historic Hawai'i Foundation, June 14, 2021.
22 Andrew Gomes, "Historic Chinatown commercial building slated for residential use," Honolulu Star-Advertiser, July 19, 2021.
23 Max Rodriguez, "Plans to convert office space into condos in Downtown Honolulu," Hawaii News Now, March 28, 2023.

24 Jake Indursky, "Developers Are Betting Big On Honolulu's Business District. Will It Pay Off?" Honolulu Civil Beat, July 20, 2023.
25 Jessica Lall, Marie Rumsey, Michael Shilstone, et al., "Adaptive Reuse: Reimagining Our City's Buildings to Address Our Housing, Economic and Climate Crises," Central City Association of Los Angeles, April 2021, p. 9.
26 Ibid.
27 Andrew Gomes, "Downtown Honolulu's Queen Emma Building to become affordable housing," Honolulu Star-Advertiser, July 13, 2018; and Janis Magin, "Work to convert Honolulu's 'Pimple Building' to affordable rentals to start soon," Pacific Business News, April 24, 2019.
28 Renee Ing, "Adaptive Reuse Of Empty Buildings Could Create Affordable Housing," Honolulu Civil Beat, Dec. 16, 2022.
29 Jason Ward and Daniel Schwam, "Can Adaptive Reuse of Commercial Real Estate Address the Housing Crisis in Los Angeles?" RAND Corp., 2022, p. 10.
30 Ibid, p. 5.
31 Lall, Rumsey, Shilstone, et al., "Adaptive Reuse: Reimagining Our City's Buildings to Address Our Housing, Economic and Climate Crises," p. 10.
32 Ward and Schwam, "Can Adaptive Reuse of Commercial Real Estate Address the Housing Crisis in Los Angeles?" p. 16.
33 William Riggs and Forrest Chamberlain, "The TOD and smart growth implications of the LA adaptive reuse ordinance," Sustainable Cities and Society, Vol. 38, April 2018.
34 David Garcia and Elliot Kwon, "Adaptive Reuse Challenges and Opportunities in California," Terner Center for Housing Innovation, University of California at Berkeley, November 2021, p. 2.
35 Hawaii County Code, Section 25-4-51. Required number of parking spaces., accessed Oct. 10, 2023; Revised Ordinances of Honolulu, § 21-6.20 Off-street parking requirements, accessed Oct. 10, 2023; Maui Code of Ordinances, 19.36B.020 - Designated number of off-street parking spaces., accessed Oct. 10, 2023; and Kauai County Code, § 8-4.5, Standards of Development Applicable to All Residential Development and § 8-6.3 Development Standards for Commercial Development, accessed Oct. 24, 2023. Kauai's parking minimums also vary by community plan area.
36 City and County of Honolulu, parcel No. 210110090000, parcel No. 210130010000 and parcel No. 210140010000, for assessment year 2023, accessed Oct. 10, 2023.
37 "The Costs of Parking in Hawai'i," prepared by PBR & Associates for the Ulupono Initiative, August 2020, p. 3.
38 Ibid, p. 5.
39 Many studios in Honolulu are just larger than 300 square feet. See: "Hawaii's First Micro-Unit Rental Community Comes to Downtown Honolulu," PD&R Edge Home, Oct. 17, 2023. Likewise, some units in San Francisco are as small as 260 square feet. See: Erin Derby, "A Bright 260-Square-Foot NYC Studio Apartment Feels Much Larger," Apartment Therapy, March 17, 2021.
40 Bryan Blanc, Michael Gangi, Carol Atkinson-Palombo, et al., "Effects of Urban Fabric Changes on Real Estate Property Tax Revenue," Transportation Research Record, Vol. 2453, Iss. 1, Jan. 1, 2014.
41 "Parking Reform for a Resilient Oahu: Ordinance 20-41," City and County of Honolulu, accessed July 12, 2023, p. 2.
42 "Progress on Parking Mandates," Parking Reform Network, accessed Oct. 3, 2023.
43 Daniel Herriges, "Is Parking Reform Hurting the Poor in San Francisco?," Strong Towns, May 10, 2023.
44 Adam Millard-Ball, Jeremy West and Nazanin Rezaei, et al., "How the Built Environment Affects Car Ownership and Travel: Evidence from San Francisco Housing Lotteries," University of California Institute for Transportation Studies, August 2020.
45 Alice Lee, "'Ohana Assistance Program holds promise for more affordable housing," The Maui News, July 17, 2023.
46 "FAQs: Supplemental Dwelling Units (SDU) Proposed Administrative Rules," Hawaii Department of Hawaiian Homelands, 2021, p. 1.
47 "Accessory Dwelling Units: Expanding Affordable Housing Options in Hawai'i," Hawaii Appleseed Center for Law and Economic Justice, April 2014, p. 1.
48 "ADUs, CPRs and 'Ohana Dwellings in Hawai'i," the "Inside Hawaii Real Estate" show on ThinkTech Hawaii, Aug. 24, 2023.

49 Sandra Oshiro, "New ohana zoning has restrictions," The Honolulu Advertiser, Dec. 12, 1993.
50 "ADUs, CPRs and 'Ohana Dwellings in Hawai'i."
51 "Building Permits – January 1, 2005 through September 30, 2023," City and County of Honolulu, last updated October 9, 2023.
52 Gordon Y. K. Pang, "Second dwelling bill moves forward," Hawaii Tribune-Herald, Feb. 9, 1994; and Gordon Y. K. Pang, "Ohana bill may create an isle building boom," Hawaii Tribune-Herald, March 13, 1994.
53 Noelle Fuiji-Oride, "ADUs Seemed Like a Simple Solution to Hawai'i's Housing Crisis," Hawaii Business Magazine, June 1, 2022. The Honolulu Department of Planning and Permitting does not have computerized records of how many ADUs were permitted prior to 2000.
54 Ordinance 15-41, Bill 20 (2015), accessed Sept. 29, 2023.
55 Karen Chapple, Jake Wegmann, Farzad Mashhood, et al., "Jumpstarting the Market for Accessory Dwelling Units: Lessons Learned From Portland, Seattle and Vancouver," a report produced for the Urban Land Institute, the Terner Center for Housing Innovation at the University of California at Berkeley and the Center for Community Innovation, 2017, p. 18.
56 "State of the Market and Local Policy: Accessory Dwelling Units in the Commonwealth of Virginia," prepared by the Center for Regional Analysis at George Mason University, the Virginia Center for Housing Research at Virginia Polytechnic University and Housing Forward Virginia, November 2021, p. 8.
57 Anika Singh Lemar, "How owner-occupancy regulations are contributing to the housing crisis," Brookings Institution, Oct. 27, 2022.
58 Graham Womack, "Cities Developing Pre-Approved ADU Plans Program," ADU Magazine, accessed Oct. 17, 2023; and Anjulie Rao, "Los Angeles Is Giving Away Plans for a Pre-Approved ADU," Dwell, Aug. 3, 2023.
59 Kam Napier, "ADU bill to be signed into law, waiving application fees up to $10,000," Pacific Business News, July 21, 2016; and Chelsea Davis, "High fees could be dissuading homeowners from erecting accessory dwelling units," Hawaii News Now, June 11, 2016.
60 "Affordable Additional Rental Unit Program," Kauai County, accessed Nov. 8, 2023.
61 Kauai County Code, § 8-30.1 Additional Rental Units., accessed Nov. 13, 2023.
62 Alice Lee, "'Ohana Assistance Program holds promise for more affordable housing," The Maui News, July 17, 2023.
63 Chuck Marohn, "Strong Towns: A Bottom-Up Revolution to Rebuild American Prosperity," Wiley, 2019, pp. 5-10.
64 Monica L. Wang, Marie-Rachelle Narcisse and Pearl A. McElfish, "Higher walkability associated with increased physical activity and reduced obesity among United States adults," Obesity, Dec. 12, 2022.
65 "The Costs of the Vehicle Economy in Hawai'i," prepared for the Ulupono Initiative by ICF Incorporated LLC, Jan. 26, 2021, pp. 17-18.
66 "TheBus Fares," TheBus fare schedule as of Jan. 1, 2023, accessed Nov. 7, 2023.
67 "Maui Bus Public Transit System," fare schedule as of July 1, 2021, accessed Nov. 7, 2023. Maui adopted a free bus pass for several groups of people in September 2023. See: "Council passes bill to create fare-free bus program," MauiNow, Sept. 9, 2023.
68 "Kauai Bus Fares," County of Kauai, accessed Nov. 7, 2023.
69 "Hawai'i Island's Hele-On Bus Now Free To Ride," Big Island Video News, July 3, 2022.
70 Lori Kowaleski-Jones, Kathleen Zick, Ken R. Smith, et al., "Walkable neighborhoods and obesity: Evaluating effects with a propensity score approach," SSM – Population Health, Vol. 6, Dec. 8, 2017; Nicholas Howell, Jack V. Tu, Rahim Moineddin, et al., "Association Between Neighborhood Walkability and Predicted 10-Year Cardiovascular Disease Risk: The CANHEART (Cardiovascular Health in Ambulatory Care Research Team) Cohort," Journal of the American Heart Association, Vol. 8, No. 21, Oct. 31, 2019; and Kevin Leyden, Michael J. Hogan, Lorrain D'arcy, et al., "Walkable Neighborhoods," Journal of the American Planning Association, April 11, 2023.
71 For more discussion, see: Olivia Gonzalez and Nolan Gray, "Zoning for Opportunity: A Survey of Home-Based-Business Regulations," Center for Growth and Opportunity at Utah State University, March 11, 2020.
72 Carl Bonham and Sumner La Croix, "The Maui County Comprehensive Affordable Housing Plan: Understanding its Pros and Cons and Ideas for How to Improve It," Economic Research Organization at the University of Hawai'i, Oct. 21, 2021, pp. 4-6.

73 Revised Ordinances of Honolulu, § 21-3.70-1 Residential uses and development standards., accessed Oct. 12, 2023.

74 Someone looking to convert a single-family home to a duplex will need a building permit, of course.

75 Maui Code of Ordinances, 19.510.070 – Special use permits., accessed Oct. 12, 2023; and Ordinance 5499, formerly Bill 96, CD1, FD2 (2022), signed into law March 9, 2023.

76 See: Ordinance 5499, formerly Bill 96, CD1, FD2 (2022), signed into law March 9, 2023.

77 Rachel Inafuku, Justin Tyndall and Carl Bonham, "Measuring the Burden of Housing Regulation in Hawaii," The Economic Research Organization at the University of Hawai'i, April 14, 2022, pp. 6-7.

78 Paul Emrath, "How Government Regulation Affects the Price of a New Home," National Association of Homebuilders, Economics and Housing Policy Group, 2011, p. 5; and Adam Millsap, Samuel Staley and Vittorio Nastasi, "Assessing the Effects of Local Impact Fees and Land-use Regulations on Workforce Housing in Florida," James Madison Institute, Dec. 11, 2018, p. 19.

79 Bill 6 (2023), CD2, FD1: Relating to Professional Self-Certification, Honolulu City Council Records Collection, accessed Oct. 10, 2023.

80 "Self-Certification Program for Nevada Licensed Development Professionals," City of North Las Vegas, accessed July 12, 2023; "Self-Certification Permit Program," City of Chicago, accessed July 12, 2023; "The Self-Certification Program," City of Phoenix, accessed July 12, 2023; "Professional Certification," New York City Department of Buildings, accessed July 12, 2023; and "Mayor's Management Report," The City of New York, September 2023, p. 328.

81 Bill 6 (2023), CD2, FD1: Relating to Professional Self-Certification, Honolulu City Council Records Collection, accessed Oct. 10, 2023.

82 Dennis Hevesi, "When Builders Are Inspectors," The New York Times, Dec. 3, 2000.

83 "Mayor's Management Report," The City of New York, September 2023, p. 328; and Mimi O'Connor, "What does it mean when an architect self-certifies?" Brick Underground, March 2, 2018.

84 "Rules for the Self-Certification Permit Program," City of Chicago Department of Buildings, Dec. 23, 2019, p. 18.

85 Julissa Briseno and Jenn Boneza, "City to revoke building permit for Hanai Loop 'monster house' project," KHON2, April 11, 2023; Rick Daysog, "To slow 'monster home' construction, city revokes permit for Pacific Heights property," Hawaii News Now, March 21, 2022; and Paula Dobbyn, "Maui County Threatens Crackdown On Controversial Monster House In Napili," Honolulu Civil Beat, July 26, 2023.